GO HOME

REPLACE YOURSELF!

How to coach a leader to run your business, so you can live your dream.

MICHELLE EDWARDS

GO HOME

REPLACE YOURSELF!

ISBN-13:978-1500629168
ISBN-10:1500629162

DEDICATION

To my family:

Sofia, may you always be the smart, beautiful, leader God meant you to be. Thank you for being a joyful daughter.

David John, may you never lose your curiosity for 'how stuff works' and your brilliant sense of humor. Thank you for making me laugh.

To my husband, David, for your tireless support and never-ending love. You are truly a great leader and thank you for being my hero.

Register This Book and Get Free Updates and Free Video Training

To get free video leadership training visit:
www.return2freedom.info
or
Text your name & email to
+1 (404) 586-4029

Or scan this QR code:

CONTENTS

THE ENTREPRENEURS DREAM

"I can't change the direction of the wind, but I can adjust my sails to always reach my destination."

JIMMY DEAN

As entrepreneurs, we learn to live life on the edge.

We accept failure as a door to new opportunities. We experience awesome highs and devastating lows.

But the dream of being an entrepreneur is much more than just pushing the limits or making a living. It is for freedom and flexibility to do the things we are passionate about.

For many, being a free-spirited entrepreneur and following life passions is liberating... and then... after 5, 10, 15, 20 years, it seems impossible to recover that dream. Impossible, because now we are left running a business and freedoms are limited.

Perhaps that is why you are here, to change your life, and find a solution to the problem of replacing yourself, so you can 'go home.'

My guess is you've built a business. It pays the bills, but you realize you are spending more time managing it and less time with family, friends and other interests. You're not alone. We all want to find the time to do the things that are important to us and our future.

In working with successful companies like the Starbucks Coffee Company and the Walt Disney Company for almost two decades, I've learned you can't run a business on your own.

You need people.

You need people who are good at performing day-to-day operations. You need people who embrace your values and want to uphold them. You need people who make great decisions even when you're not around.

When you create a successful working environment with great people, you will also find the ability to *Go Home.*

You might be wondering... "How do I accomplish this? I've never trained a manager or coached a leader, and I have no idea where to begin."

I know where you are and I'm excited to introduce you to the steps used to successfully train thousands of managers. These concepts are easy to grasp for owners and leaders even if you haven't had much management training in the past.

You will discover some secrets to:

- **Creating values and guidelines**
- **Hiring and training the right people**
- **Coaching for success**
- **Follow-up and effective feedback**

These steps will improve your staff's morale, their effectiveness, and overall excellence while running your business. They'll ensure it'll run the way you want it to be run even while you're not present.

I appreciate the opportunity to share this knowledge with you. Thank you for taking the time to pick up read this book.

First, take a moment and register for some bonus materials. They are packed with useful content. Visit: www.return2freedom.info

Also, these concepts are taught and expanded upon in an ongoing monthly coaching program and community that can be found at return2freedom.com. I look forward to hearing your story as part of this collective community of entrepreneurs and leaders.

Michelle Edwards

"I help business owners teach others to take their place so they can focus on the life they want to live — even if they've never had any experience coaching & training managers before."

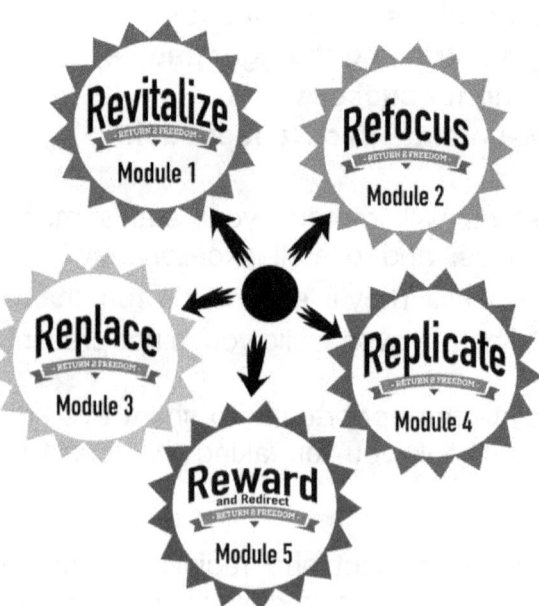

Return2Freedom

GO HOME IN 5 STEPS

"The task of the leader is to get his people from where they are to where they have not been."

HENRY A. KISSINGER

Meet Ian

Ian is a successful manager in Ohio. His journey started as a part-time employee with Starbucks.

When I met Ian 12 years ago, he was young, rode a bike to work, and wanted to create a 'Tea Passport' to help partners (employees) understand the company's tea offerings.

He was also an entomologist and had a dream of working with coffee growers at origin on sustainable organic pesticide practices.

Ian was the kind of guy who looked for opportunity

wherever he went. He was passionate about certain things and made decisions in accordance to his values.

But if you ever asked Ian about these qualities, he would probably wince and wonder how anyone would really 'see' these strengths in him.

When asked about becoming an assistant manager, Ian responded by saying, "I can't be a manager. I don't even drive. How will I ride my bike across town to work? I don't think I'm management material."

Obviously Ian wasn't confident in his abilities. He was almost legally blind and fearful of getting a driver's license. He didn't consider becoming a manager because he felt incapable of running a store.

What he didn't understand at the time was this: he had what it took to be a great manager.

After encouragement and some coaching, he eventually agreed to a promotion, and in the coming years he became one of the most successful managers I've had the privilege of working with.

So, how does this apply to you?

As an owner, when you are looking for someone to manage and run your business, take a look at those around you who are already on your team. You may find a 'diamond in the rough,' someone who will grow into a great manager.

Ian may not have had the confidence at first to lead. However, his skills of decision making, solution seeking for fellow employees, being a team player, and providing excellence in customer service were behaviors needed in successful leadership.

But wait, there is more to Ian's story...

In time, Ian expressed a desire to become a district manager, which created a gateway to teach him a new skill.

A skill many owners and leaders realize must be sharpened, for themselves and those who manage for them.

Leading others through influence.

You see, as a store manager in retail, it's easy to roll up your sleeves and mop the floors, take the orders, call a customer or put together a schedule.

However, as a district manager you no longer have a direct impact on the business because of your physical presence. You must rely on the people that work within the store to accomplish operational tasks. The only way to guide them is through your influence and coaching.

In the same way, any leader must transition from managing and running a business to influencing others to run it for him.

Ian and I then began to talk about the idea of leading through influence and handing over many tasks to his store staff. There were a few tasks he would not be able to delegate because of his position, but overall his staff were able to accomplish most operational goals without his physical presence.

The goal was to give his team the duties of store operations and continue to provide specific praise and feedback to keep them on the right path.

Secondly, he needed to look for areas of opportunity outside of his store. Together we outlined a plan to 'replace himself' in his store, so he could influence and serve in other capacities.

In several months, his team successfully continued store operations without his physical presence. He was able to go to other locations and help new managers, participate in more community projects by volunteering his time, and was recognized by city organizers and elected as a board member. His leadership and influence had reached far beyond the counter of his store.

So, as a business owner or leader, how do you become successful at coaching people when you have so many other things to deal with? How can you replicate Ian's journey of success?

Let's dive into a simple solution that will help you 'replace yourself' — so you can 'go home'.

5 STEPS TO REPLACE YOURSELF

1. Revitalize ~ Set Up A Culture

Employees and leaders need a compass and core values provide exactly that: a guide to help align their decisions with what is most crucial to the organization.

This is more than a mission statement hanging on a wall, it's a set of real principles that will help your team know and understand the expectations.

Teaching leaders to use these core values is essential to building a culture that will help employees excel in the workplace and positively impact brand reputation.

2. Refocus ~ Prioritize Duties

Communicating tasks and ideas that matter most is vital to execution and exceeding goals. You not only teach how to communicate these expectations, but come alongside to help formulate them as well.

When your team knows the priorities, it's easier for them to exceed expectations. Also, by following your lead, leaders can embrace your values and priorities to provide consistency in operations and interpersonal relations.

3. Replace ~ Choose Great People

You can't be everywhere all of the time. In order to focus on other priorities away from your business, you need a leader who can run things for you when you're not around.

It's important to identify the leader you need and the team of individuals that will help everyone be successful.

4. Replicate ~ Teach How To Coach

Coaching and training can be used throughout the organization with every employee. Once you have set up guidelines, it's time to teach your leader how to coach and run the business by delegating and teaching others.

Also, through coaching, a leader will begin to achieve success in several areas of personal development and people management.

5. Redirect and Reward ~ Proper Feedback

Praise and follow-up will ultimately be the only tasks required of you as a business owner after the previous steps have been accomplished.

At this point, your leader in charge becomes the person accountable for the overall operations of the business, and the one you communicate with the most.

These steps will also reward those that meet and

exceed expectations, and of course; redirect any behavior that may need adjustment.

How would your life change if praise and the occasional follow up is all employees needed from you? Would you be able to find some time to schedule important networking opportunities or that much needed time with family?

That's what the Return2Freedom community is all about. To help you teach a leader how to run your business and be successful, so you can live your dream as an entrepreneur.

For more detailed steps on how to make this a reality … keep reading.

Step 1 ~ REVITALIZE

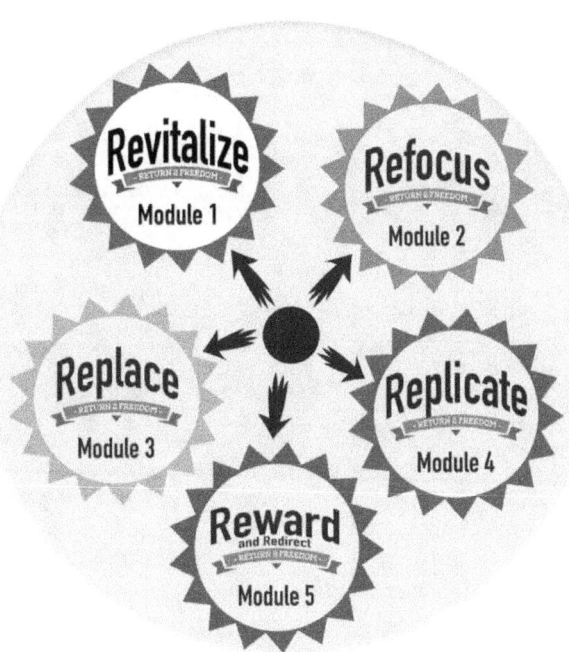

REVITALIZE WITH CULTURE

"Define what your brand stands for, its core values and tone of voice, and then communicate consistently in those terms."

SIMON MAINWARING

World Class Culture with Core Values

All major companies have a mission statement or set of guiding principles. Let's call them 'core values.' Core values are used to communicate the purpose and vision of the organization and act as guidelines for employees to use when they make decisions on behalf of the company.

Before you train and coach someone to take your place, think of what values you would like your team to embrace within your business.

Values are different from policies and procedures.

Policies and procedures ensure safety, product quality, lawful operations, etc. Core values however, help your team make principled decisions even if it means breaking a policy.

Let me give you an example, when I worked for the Disney Store, in New York City, one of our policies was to not allow guests/customers in the storage room area, or as we called it, 'backstage'.

This policy provided safety and security for guests and staff, and to be honest, the area itself wasn't very magical. It had particle board shelves, stored products, hard floors and industrial lighting.

Our goal was to create magical moments for guests and the storage room was not the kind of place for a magical moment. Still, when a mom came up to me and asked if her son could use the employee restroom located in the backstage area, I had a choice to make.

I could stick to the policy and tell her, "I'm sorry we don't have a public restroom," and send her out on the street to look for one or I could align with our guiding principles and make a better decision by allowing the parent to take their child to the restroom.

To help give you some perspective, this was one of the statements in the company mission:

"We are dedicated to exceeding our guest's expectations by providing an authentic Disney

retail experience through excellence in service, product, and show."
~ excerpt from The Disney Store Inc. Mission Statement 1998

At that moment, the guest's expectation was clear. She needed a restroom for her child. The policy said otherwise, but I knew it was more important to break the policy this time, follow the mission, and allow them in the back room area.

I explained to the parent how the storage room wasn't as 'magical' as the front, but I would be happy to escort them to the restroom and back.

Of course, the parent and the child were happy and I did my best to stay true to the guidelines of our mission statement. Looking back on this experience, I realize how important it was for the company to provide me with a mission in order to make wise decisions.

A company's values are sometimes trumped by policies.

Let me begin this next story by stating that I have chosen to keep the name of this company a secret. We all have had bad service experiences and it is not always a direct reflection of the company. My purpose is not to expose a company but to reflect on how important it is to train leadership well.

I had purchased a pair of water shoes for my three

year old son from a 'big box' retail store, he wasn't with me in the store, so I was unable to let him try them on before I bought them.

As soon as I returned home, I put the water shoes on him and he walked down our sidewalk to the car. He said, "My feet hurt," in his little voice. So, I checked the shoes and said, "These don't fit. Do they? We can't go to the pool with these."

I took them off immediately and the next day I brought them back to the store to exchange them for a larger pair.

When I arrived at the store, I went to the customer service desk, gave them my receipt, the water shoes, and asked if I could exchange them for a larger size.

The employee looked at the shoes, saw the dirt on the bottom of the white soles and said, "I'm sorry we can't return or exchange these — they have been worn."

Naturally, I explained what had happened and how the water shoes didn't fit. I knew she was doing her best to follow company policy, but I still asked if there was another solution. I figured she would just return them for me so I (the customer) would be happy in the end.

"No, I'm sorry we can't return these shoes," was her response.

At which point, I asked for a manager who could honor my request. To my surprise, after explaining the situation again, the manager insisted the shoes couldn't be exchanged and if I had any further questions or concerns, I could call the 800 number or use the store's guest courtesy phone.

I must confess, that my behavior in the next moment was not something I'm proud of. I became frustrated and went on to say something like, "It is sad you work for a company that doesn't trust you to make good decisions on behalf of the customer." Then, I continued with some crazy rant about how unfair it was for the company to put her in a position to deal with angry customers and give her no authority to resolve their issues.

I was livid. Partly because I've taught managers to find resolutions in these situations and I didn't understand how a 'big box retail chain' could screw up a $10 return so badly.

I've also dealt with similar customer issues on a regular basis and know the lifetime value of a customer is so much more important than this policy.

Well, I left the water shoes on the counter feeling as though I had been cheated out of $10. Of course, I went over to the courtesy phone, only to be greeted by a message, from the customer service department telling me, that all agents were busy and I could leave a message.

Well, <insert sigh here> I left a message ... a duplicate rant about putting the customer first. I'm sure I was a topic around the water cooler at lunch time.

Have you ever had a moment when you just didn't want to 'give in' to a customer because of a policy or principle? Or have you ever had a bad service experience where you wished you could talk with a manager that would listen and resolve your issue?

In this case, the manager's decision making process was impeeded by her focus on the policy and not on the company values of excellent service.

Unfortunately, it is not all the manager's fault. Upper management failed to provide the right environment for her to make decisions on behalf of her customers.

How do I know this with certainty? When given the choice, an employee will do whatever they can to keep a customer from getting angry. It makes the day go smoothly. It's a natural reaction.

However, a good manager will act in accordance with their coaching. Apparently, the coaching she had received was, "Stick to the policies no matter what."

When employees are given training to keep in mind the lifetime value of a customer and align themselves with the values and principles of the company — everyone wins! Customers are happier, employees feel good and exceed expectations, and business flourishes because word of mouth gets around.

DID YOU KNOW THAT 95% OF CONSUMERS SHARE THEIR BAD SERVICE EXPERIENCES AND 50% OF THOSE SHARE THEM MORE THAN FIVE TIMES, INCLUDING SOCIAL MEDIA & ONLINE REVIEWS? *ZENDESK/MARKETINGCHARTS.COM

Before there were online reviews, unsatisfied customers would write and send emails or letters to companies about their experiences.

As managers, we were coached that for every person writing a letter about service or a product, there was an average of 25 other customers that didn't take the time to tell us the same thing.

In our connected world, it is so much easier to state an opinion and share it online. Customers are plugged in and can see reviews from everywhere - Facebook, Google, Twitter, Yelp .... My friends, family and the rest of the world see what I think. And I can know what they think too.

Because good and bad reviews are easily seen, it makes perfect sense for a company to establish values and ask employees to align with them when making decisions.

Let me end these thoughts with this positive story:

I would frequent an outdoor mall near our home in Dublin, Ohio. One of my favorite places to shop was Nordstrom. Especially for my kids' shoes.

They had a coloring station and balloons for the kids, so shopping there for shoes was more enjoyable than traditional shoe stores.

The employees always helped me find the right fit for my little ones, no matter how many times we asked to try on another selection. The shoe quality was so good the shoes would last until they needed a new size, which was always a plus.

One particular visit was when my daughter was only 2 1/2. As you can imagine, it's difficult to tell whether or not shoes fit comfortably at that age. But, after measuring and trying on several pairs of shoes, my daughter finally settled on a pair of slip-on tennis shoes.

It was the first time she chose a pair of slip-on sneakers, but I wanted to encourage her independence, and these were shoes she could put on and take off by herself. So we opted for a pink style and off we went.

About a month later, I went to pick my daughter up from daycare and the teacher explained that she thought my daughter's shoes were bothering her. Each day she would take them off only to reluctantly put them back on when it was time to go out to the playground.

Knowing her shoes were uncomfortable, the next weekend we headed back to Nordstrom, to buy a new pair of shoes that fit comfortably.

As I approached the counter, I showed the employee my daughter's shoes and explained that they were bothering her and asked if she could help me find a new pair.

After testing several pairs, we finally decided on a pair of traditional lace-up sneakers and my little lady was running around proudly in her new 'light up' shoes.

As I went up to the counter to pay for the new shoes, the employee said she would be happy to exchange the old shoes for the new ones.

I couldn't believe it! I was so pleasantly surprised that I decided from that day on, I would always buy my kids' shoes at Nordstrom. I even persuaded my friends to shop there for their kids' shoes.

Here is the mission of Nordstrom:

"NORDSTROM'S COMMITMENT
In store or online, wherever new opportunities arise—Nordstrom works relentlessly to give customers the most compelling shopping experience possible. The one constant? John W. Nordstrom's founding philosophy: offer the customer the best possible service, selection, quality and value."

So let me ask you, do you think the employee upheld the mission of Nordstrom? When you think about the two shoe stories... what decision do you think your employees would have made if presented with my dilemmas?

What would your style of leadership permit them to do when making decisions while you're not around?

One of my favorite leaders, Joe Dallaqua, used to say, "People vote with their pocketbooks."

I'll vote and shop at the stores that take care of me as a customer. It is so vital that the leadership of a business use these kinds of opportunities to create small victories for their reputation and brand.

These moments increase loyalty, but most importantly cheat the other retailers out of $$$ because customers won't go anywhere else.

Now, I know there are policies in place for safety, security, etc, so I'm not saying we throw *all* policies out the window.

Instead, I will proclaim that core values are vital to business. Employees can use them to make better decisions on behalf of company for their customers. Surprisingly enough, the values of the companies I've worked for were about people.

I recently read an article where the Disney stores changed their mission to: "The Best 30 Minutes of a Child's Day."*

When you take a moment to think about it, their values are all wrapped up in that one statement: The Best 30 Minutes in a Child's Day.

If it is truly their mission, then the cast members of each team know that whatever it takes, their job is to create the best 30 minutes of a child's day.

When employees need to make decisions, and they are not exactly sure what the outcome should be, they can always look to the values of the company and ask themselves, "Does this decision align with the mission?"

In my experience, the managers who align their decisions with the values of the company were the most successful managers. They knew what the goals were and they knew the core values of the company could guide them.

So to give your business a running start, create some guiding principles or core values that are important to you and your business. Promote them to your staff.

Frame them or make them part of employee orientation or add them to your employee packet. Most importantly teach your staff to use them as guidelines when policies fail. And, you will find that it's very easy for an employee or manager to make decisions once they are confident in holding true to your core values.

Warning: If your core values become just a plaque hanging on the wall and are not lived out in day-to-day activities then that's all they will become — just a plaque on the wall.

Ensure the culture in your company supports the core values you create, as they will allow your employees to make decisions on a daily basis without you being present.

For inspiration in creating values and a culture for your business, I recommend visiting the online websites for Starbucks, Disney and Nordstrom to see their current mission statements.

Step 2 ~ REFOCUS

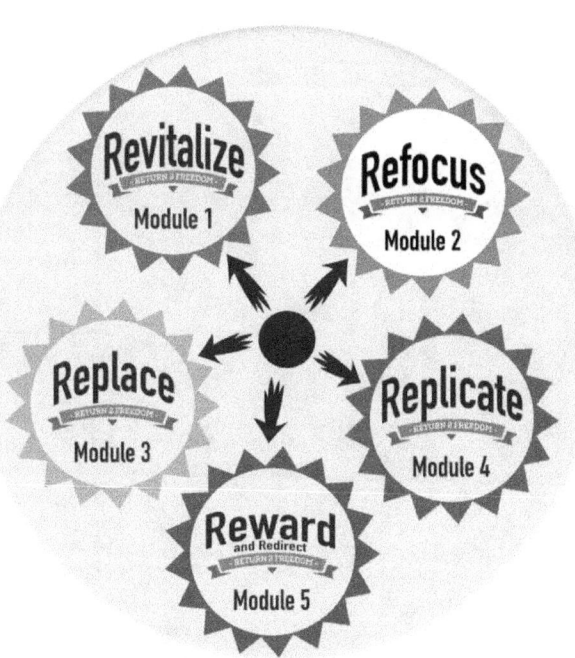

REFOCUS - YOUR PRIORITIES

"Good things happen when you get your priorities straight."

SCOTT CAAN

CHOOSING YOUR PRIORITIES

We've already established your core values will help your team make decisions while you are not around. **Your priorities can also give understanding and direction on which tasks to accomplish first.**

Priorities are driven by what matters most.

During my time at Starbucks, the most important policy was called — the 'Just say "YES"' policy.'

There were many tasks that needed to be accomplished to keep the store running smoothly. However, it was this policy that kept employees focused on what mattered most: the customer.

This policy made it easy for employees to simply say, 'yes' and fulfill customer requests while they were busy managing the business. In turn, this built brand loyalty and added to the bottom line.

While it may sound crazy, most of the time, customers didn't have extravagant requests like a free espresso machine. They usually wanted a little extra syrup in their coffee or a warmed bagel.

Consider the lifetime value of a customer.

Here's a little exercise:

1. Take the average dollar amount a customer spends in your business over the course of a year.

2. Multiply that by how many years on average they will continue using your services or consuming your products.

For example: Take a typical coffee shop that is located in the heart of town next to a commuter bus stop. Say they sell a large coffee for $3.00.

A commuter purchasing a large coffee 5 days a week and perhaps twice a month on weekends when visiting downtown will spend $852 a year on their coffee alone.

Item	Purchased	Total retail
$3.00 coffee	x 5 days	$15.00 week
		$780.00 year
$3.00 coffee	x 2 weekends mth	$6.00 additional
		+ $72.00 year
Total:		$852.00 year
Lifetime Value	x 10 years	$8520.00

Let's say the customer lives in the area and continues to work at the job where he takes the commuter bus for 10 years before he moves away.

Add on a bagel here and there or a pound of coffee to take home and you have a customer that will spend around $1,100 a year in that coffee shop.

In this example, the lifetime value of this customer is somewhere between $8,520 and $11,000 dollars.

Consider this...

If every day he pays for his coffee but before leaving asks for an extra shot of syrup, in his cup, what is more profitable? Saying, 'yes' to the customer every day, or 'no'?

In order to continue employing people and servicing customers, it's important that there are policies and procedures in place to help the coffee shop remain profitable. These policies may include ringing in customer orders, charging appropriate prices, managing inventory and maintaining health and safety standards.

Employee's want to meet expectations and if an employee was taught that an added shot of syrup to a cup of coffee has an extra charge, they will 'stick to the policy and ask the customer to pay for the extra syrup, because they believe they are doing the right thing.

But, what if every time the employee upholds the policy they are at risk of losing the customer? Can the owner afford that?

You may be wondering what this has to do with priorities. So, let us make the connection.

You see, in my opinion, the 'Just say Yes' policy is a priority that has safe guarded future business and helped employees make decisions on behalf of the customer. Remember, the lifetime value of a customer is much more valuable than an extra shot of syrup.

Likewise, your most important policy or priority should enable your leader make decisions that you will be proud of.

Your employees still need to know what tasks need to be done, how to do them, and most importantly what motivates you.

Take a moment and think about the tasks you would focus on first if you didn't have the responsibilities of running the business — just managing it.

Outline five or six duties that are vitally important to you and your business. The challenge now is to rank those items accordingly.

Communicating Priorities

If you owned a gift-shop and you were asked to prioritize the following items, in what order would you list them?

- Customer Service
- Cleanliness
- Quality of products
- Operational tasks
- Safety and Security

Tough isn't it? They all seem important. See, there are certain times when one task will take precedence over the other.

For instance, if there aren't any customers to help and employees are looking for things to do, cleanliness or operational tasks may be most important. Or, if a customer walks in the door, then attending to the customer would come first. If this customer passes out on the floor unconscious, I would venture to say, safety and security rises to the top.

Each part of the day or circumstance will require some guidelines in order to help your team know what to do and when. If cleanliness is the first thing you think about when you walk into your establishment, then your team needs to know it's important to you.

If customers are more important than cleanliness, then communicate it and trust your team to take care of customers before they start the cleaning duties. When your team has a crazy, busy day, understand they may not able to do everything on the list. But, importantly, they'll know which tasks can wait and where to put their focus first.

At Disney, our focus was to create magical moments for our guests (customers). So when making decisions in the store, it was very easy to prioritize tasks, because those related to customer service needed to come first.

Perhaps it was smiling and greeting our guests or stocking shelves with product or making sure the register tape was full so we wouldn't run out during a rush.

Do you see how it made our daily decision-making much easier? We would schedule non-customer related tasks after the former had been attended to.

An embarrassing moment...

New York City was a high-profile market for the company and several times a year product buyers from different departments would fly out from California to see how their items were presented and sold.

They also asked for feedback on the fixtures that were housing the products, customer comments and any concerns we had.

These were always fun visits, but they were also nerve-racking too. The most important thing to these visitors was their little niche in the store, and my priorities were more about the overall operation of the store and not just one area.

However, when we prepared for these visits, we did our best to pay careful attention to the buyers' area before they came to visit.

Except this one time....

I was informed that the novelty department was flying from California to pick our brain and see their products. I left instructions for my team to ensure we had a great presentation for them.

The problem? I didn't tell them exactly what the priority area was. As they finished closing duties, my manager explained in a note to me that there was just one area left to stock in the morning.

Well, wouldn't you know, of course, it was the novelty items that were left empty. Our visitors arrived bright and early, before we had time to fill the fixtures.

I was so embarrassed. The buyer team had flown in to 'see' the beautiful displays of their products only to find half empty shelves and bins.

If I had taken the time to tell my team to stock those shelves first before they did their usual tasks, there would have been no question as to what was most important to me and the company at that moment.

You see the visitors from corporate in the story probably wouldn't have even noticed if the carpet had not been vacuumed or if we failed to dust the front of the store.

And that is what we sometimes do as owners. We forget to communicate what is important and then get irritated when an employee does everything else but the one thing we wanted them to do.

In order to help your leader manage and meet your expectations set them up for success by communicating the most important priorities.

Isn't it easier to do everything myself?

Have you ever seen a restaurant manager try to be a bus boy, server and hostess all at once? This is exactly what happened when visiting a restaurant with my family for the first time.

I didn't expect to find this perfect example of what happens to a business owners' countenance and that of their team, when they fail to communicate what's most important.

First, while eating my dinner, I couldn't help but notice the servers. They stood near the edge of the room watching the owner running around doing different tasks in the restaurant — seemingly afraid to interrupt him.

Every few moments he would snap his fingers and wave his hand at an employee, and they would go to the table he motioned them to. He hurriedly bussed tables, grumbling under his breath. It was extremely uncomfortable, but then again I'm not sure any other customers noticed besides me.

I imagined how helpless his employees felt and how exhausted he must have been every night when he went home.

If only the owner understood that if he just took the time to communicate the most important tasks and expectations to his team and followed-up with a question like, "Is there anything I can do for you?" or "How can I help?", It would make every shift run more smoothly, and the end result would be a team confident in their job who know how to meet the expectations.

In a recent survey, 'America's Workforce: A Revealing Account of What US Employees Really Think About Today's Workplace,' the results were consistent with what employees have wanted for decades.

Although many would argue that pay rates are most important to employees, the reality is they want to 'be in on things': to have a part of the vision of where the company is going. They want to trust upper management to be authentic and communicate the direction. Lastly, they want on the job training and development so they can be better at their job.

All too often, owners are stressed out with the pressures of the business and they forget the people standing around them just waiting for the opportunity to pitch in and add value to the business.

Create some priorities for your leadership team and communicate what's most important to you. This will ensure that if all the tasks aren't completed you and your team will know they did the most important things first.

Step 3 ~ REPLACE

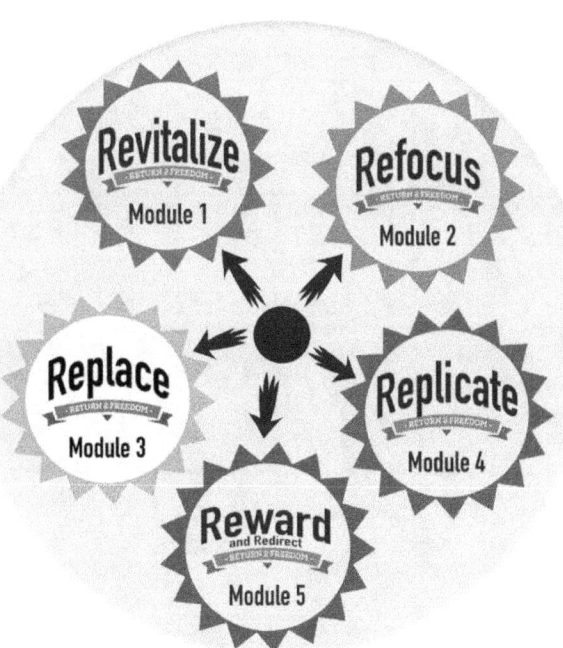

REPLACE - FIND YOUR DIAMOND

"In the past a leader was a boss. Today's leaders must be partners with their people... they no longer can lead solely based on positional power."

KEN BLANCHARD

THE LEADER YOU NEED

I was around 20 years old when I was given the keys to a multimillion dollar business.

It was my job to schedule, hire employees, train them to receive shipments, turn on the lights, count the money, stock the shelves, keep everyone safe and to lock up at night.

Through the years, I've been a part of taking over new teams, re-building existing ones, and coaching leaders to manage.

If there is one thing in common with successful teams, it's the caliber of people that comprises them.

What makes a good leader? It's someone you can trust to run your business the way you want it to be run.

Right now, you may be thinking about the kind of person you would like to take over for you. In your mind is a list of criteria and character traits you would like to see in that person. Perhaps, it's someone who is always on time or a person with a positive attitude.

Chances are you've tried to find these qualities in individuals before. Usually, the list of traits we would like to have in an employee, comes from the things we didn't like about those we have hired in the past.

You may even feel it's impossible to find a good hire. Don't lose hope, you're not alone.

In the following pages, I've outlined a simple formula designed to help you find the right leader (your diamond). A leader who will be able to run and manage things for you. You want someone who can earn your trust and the trust of your employees.

There are 3 behaviors to look for in a leader.

When you look for a leader, there are also qualities

you can't teach. They are the character qualities that are part of a person's being. A leader, you can trust, will make good decisions even without a leadership role. Perhaps you would consider someone within your team to take over this management position.

If you have someone already within the organization, they could take over for you in as little as 4 months with right coaching.

Behavior 1 ~ Someone willing to go the extra mile.

This idea originally came from ancient Rome. Roman soldiers could ask any person of Jewish decent to carry their backpack for them. Under the law, this person couldn't refuse and was required to carry the pack for a mile. In the biblical story, Jesus asked his followers to be willing to go a second mile even though the law did not require it.

Do you know of someone who is willing to go the extra mile, a person ready to seize opportunity and take action? Do you know a person willing to do more for others than what's expected of them just because it's who they are?

Let me give you an illustration of this:

Nate, a shift supervisor, working at Starbucks, received a call from a customer who needed his help. The customer explained that he and his wife were closing on a house later that day and the time of the meeting had changed.

After several failed attempts to reach her, he called Starbucks, because it was located right around the corner from where his wife worked.

He asked Nate if someone could take his wife's favorite coffee drink to her, with a message to call him. Without hesitation, Nate agreed. He made the beverage, walked down the block, and hand-delivered the tasty beverage with the important message.

A few days later, this customer contacted me to retell his story. He explained how impressed he was with Nate's quick response and mentioned his wife was able to connect with him and the closing on the house went smoothly thanks to Nate's assistance.

It wasn't Nate's job to run around the corner and deliver a message. In fact his responsibility was to make sure the doors were open, coffee was brewing, and customers were happy within the store.

In this instance, he saw an opportunity and provided the solution for a customer. He did it because he knew it was the right thing to do. He knew the benefits would far outweigh the costs.

As his district manager, I couldn't have been more delighted with his decision. It was guaranteed that through his actions, Nate secured a life long customer that day.

He not only received unsolicited positive comments from the customer, he was also recognized by the company, thanking him for his excellence in service. Nate works for Apple now and wishes one day to be a training manager.

I don't know about you, but I would love to have a guy like that training my employees.

Behavior 2 ~ Someone who has a positive effect on everyone around them.

Have you ever worked with a grump or a person who always complains about things and is rarely cheerful about life or circumstances? These are not the characteristics of a leader.

I brought this up because sometimes we have long time employees we might consider for leadership because they know how to do everything. But, we've forgotten how others perceive them. They are jaded with life and like working with us because it's too much trouble to do something else. If you are looking to place an individual already on your team in leadership be sure they are the right person for the position.

You are looking for someone who likes to see the glass half full and not half empty. (at least most of the time)

A good leader is someone who positively impacts employees and customers just by being themselves.

They are enthusiastic about change and optimizing systems. They create an environment that's enjoyable for customers and employees.

They enjoy the challenge of new tasks, accept responsibility for their own learning, and often take a problem-solving approach to difficulties or issues.

They are honest about problems or issues and offer solutions or suggestions to help.

Ultimately, this individual wants to be a team player, wants to help out where they can and needs some affirmation they are on the right track. You can probably see how this person will spark unsolicited positive comments from their colleagues or customers.

Behavior 3 ~ Someone who gets unsolicited positive comments from co-workers & customers.

In a high growth company, employees want to be promoted to continue their career. Often these employees want a list of things they need to do in order to be promoted.

As a district manager, I had many conversations with individuals who wanted to be promoted. They would ask, "What do I need to do?"

Much to their surprise, these three behaviors were

what we would discuss. This last one was always the hardest behavior to discuss because it relied on their influence and relationships with others.

To embrace this idea was challenging for them because it was more about who they should be and less about what they would do. It was the one behavior they could not control. They could only work toward teamwork and becoming the influencer they so wished to be.

The key words here are: unsolicited positive comments.

When I visited stores and people would share with me how they enjoyed working with another employee or customers would go out of there way to speak highly of a barista or manager, it would inspire me to keep an eye on those employees.

Look for a leader who has all three of these qualities, so you can hand the keys of your business over and go home worry free.

Interviewing to find a leader.

If you don't have the right candidate to fill this leadership role, it's time to interview. Speaking from experience, for every 10-15 interviews you will find two people who have the qualities you are looking for.

So, needless to say, it may take several interviews

before you find the person you would consider hiring.

A typical hiring process goes like this:

Most business owners receive a resumé and look at experience and references to see if the candidate would be good for the position. Then, during the interview they often talk about job responsibilities, wages and some expectations of the position. Next, they ask the candidate if they can do the job and how soon can they start.

Does this sound familiar? This process seems perfectly fine, but it doesn't help you determine whether or not the candidate would be a good leader for you or your team. Instead, interview with the intent to look for behaviors that will be needed to lead.

Recent past behavior is the best predictor of future behavior.

Diamonds require some digging and inspection to prove their value. The same due diligence is required when hiring a leader.

To change up the interview process and make it more effective, you will ask questions that bring out answers pointing to recent past behaviors.

I have enclosed some great interview questions on the next page. Here are some guidelines for conducting the interview.

First, interview in a comfortable environment where you can sit face to face with the candidate.

Second, look over the application and resumé if applicable.

Third, ask questions in a conversation like manner. Remember to allow the candidate to speak 90% of the time.

Fourth, ensure lawful conversation. Do not ask personal questions pertaining to family, kids, etc.

The questions I asked in every interview:

1. *I see here you worked at _____ tell me a little about your experience there.*

2. *What did you like most and the least about your position there?*

3. *What three words would your best friend use to describe you?*

4. *Tell me about a time when you gave excellent customer service (or exceeded a company's expectation).*

5. *What do others give you feedback on that you could improve?*

6. *Right now, what are you doing for your own personal development?*

7. *Tell me about a time where you broke policy in the workplace. What was the policy and why did you break it?*

8. *Have you ever had to deal with an angry customer or vendor? If so, describe the situation... and what did you do?*

9. *Have you ever been given a task of organizing a team toward a goal? How did you gain support and was it successful? What would you do differently next time?*

10. *Tell me about an accomplishment you've achieved and are most proud of.*

11. *Who is the very best boss or teacher you've ever had and why were they so great?*

After asking these questions and assessing their answers, determine from the answers whether or not they would be a good fit for your team.

If so, now is the time to review the position responsibilities and compensation, as well as answer any questions they may have.

Interview evaluation

During the interview, look for red flags, anything that doesn't jive with you. Make a note for further inquiry if needed.

Let's say, the way they handled an irate customer did not meet your expectations, don't hire them. They will not change patterns of behavior or thought processes fast enough to be the leader to replace you.

If they said something negative about their past workplace, chances are, their opinion won't change that much within your workplace. It's just who they are. They will find something negative no matter where they work. Accept it and move on, there are other candidates for you.

You might be thinking, "Well, sometimes people just get stuck into a bad situation; I can understand why they would complain about it..."

Yes, there are times when people get stuck in a bad workplace situation..., but a person with integrity and much to offer will not dwell on that. They will instead focus on other things during the interview and try to remain positive about their past experience even though it may have been dreadful.

Here's something to keep in mind:

During an interview they are at their best and if you aren't impressed, it will only go downhill after they have been hired. If they are not a good fit, complete the interview and move on.

But, if the person is right for you, go back to your list of qualities and ask yourself, "Does this person meet my expectations?" If all signs are saying, 'YES' ask another employee to interview them also.

Why have another employee interview the candidate?

First, it will be invaluable for the new hire to meet someone in the workplace, it helps with their transition into your team. Second, you'll be able to get some feedback from an employee's perspective, because they are not 'the boss,' they may get a different 'performance' from the candidate.

Also, those that work for you already know what it takes to do the job. They usually can decipher from their conversation whether this person would be up for the challenge. Lastly, the candidate may have additional questions about the workplace that your employee can answer.

The interview with your employee will not be as lengthy as the one you conduct, perhaps only three or four questions. It is a great opportunity to see the candidate in a different light, and it gives you a chance to empower your employees to be a part of the decision-making process.

Interview on a regular basis for a while, at least once

a month for six months to get the hang of it. Take a day and schedule three interviews if possible.

Then you will get into a groove and start to understand, through repetition, what answers you are looking for from the candidates. After a few months, you will be asking questions, evaluating answers and gaining insight rather quickly when interviewing someone for your team.

Plan staffing needs out a few months or even a year ahead of time. Continue to interview as you go... even if you don't think you have any positions to fill... because the unexpected always happens, and you may need to hire a candidate sooner than you anticipated.

Due diligence is required when checking references. Try to get at least three, more if possible. Character references are a great way to speak with someone who knows the candidate well.

Everyone has a strength.

Some digging is required to find a diamond and your diamond may not be a perfect match.

You may already have someone in mind. You may be looking for someone just like you. Someone who will do everything exactly like you do it. This is not your goal.

A word of caution: No one will ever be able to run the business exactly the way you run the business. Believe it or not, it just might be a good thing for your business because each leader will have different strengths.

I've trained many managers and have seen people who have different strengths become a great influence in the lives of those around them. And they are not all cut from the same cloth. It takes people with seemingly opposing perspectives to leverage each others' strengths and accomplish great things. It takes teamwork.

Let me explain with a little story:

Scott, a fellow district manager, and I had the task of opening almost 20 stores within a few years. There is much to do when opening shops at that rate.

The challenge: He and I did not always see things the same way.

Now, Scott's background was from the military and a highly driven company prior to working with Starbucks. My experience was with Disney, and before that I traveled with an international ministry, out of California, doing mission work.

So, as you can imagine, we approached challenges from different perspectives. For a while it seemed like oil and water trying to get along to complete the tasks at hand.

Then, we attended a two day leadership training conference held by our regional director, Joe. This team building meeting changed the way Scott and I worked together.

A facilitator took us through a personality test called DISC.* You may be familiar with this test and the outcome for our team was phenomenal. During this process, I learned Scott was a 'driver'. A person who when given the challenge of getting to the other side of a brick wall would just charge right through it.

I, on the other hand, when faced with the same challenge would cheer everyone on to help each

---

Personality traits described in the DISC evaluation:

D   Dominance
Results Oriented, Bottom Line Philosophy, Confidence ~ Big Picture Minded, Straightforward, Likes Challenge

I   Influence
Persuades Others, Open, Relationship Oriented, Enthusiastic, Optimistic, Desires Collaboration,

S   Steadiness
Cooperation is Key, Sincere, Dependable, Approaches Challenge Calmly, Supportive, Humble

C   Conscientiousness
Accurate, Objective, Likes Independence, Detailed Oriented, Competent, Expert

* See Resources for more info.

---

other get over the wall and to the other side.

We found that our leader Joe would analyze the wall before crafting a plan and others on our team would be more systematic looking for a system others could replicate to get to the other side.

You see, we began to understand which perspective each of us came from and why we would respond differently to the same challenge. Understanding our differences, helped us grow and perform better as a team.

Scott and I learned to use this knowledge as we continued to work together. When there were tasks that needed to be immediately accomplished, Scott was the one who spearheaded the project. When we needed to persuade our team to get on board with a new direction, I was on point to be the cheerleader to get everyone ready to go.

It was an incredible lessoned learned that I continue to use each time I am given a task or challenge to overcome.

Use this proven practice to embrace other's strengths and leverage them to accomplish a project or challenge.

Just keep in mind, you are always looking for good, talented, energetic people. Hire diversity in your team. You'll want leaders, cheerleaders, analyzers and stabilizers.

Everyone has a strength, and when you have a diverse team it allows you to pull from their strengths to manage daily operations and keep the business running smoothly. After you find your diamond it's time to coach.

Step 4 ~ REPLICATE

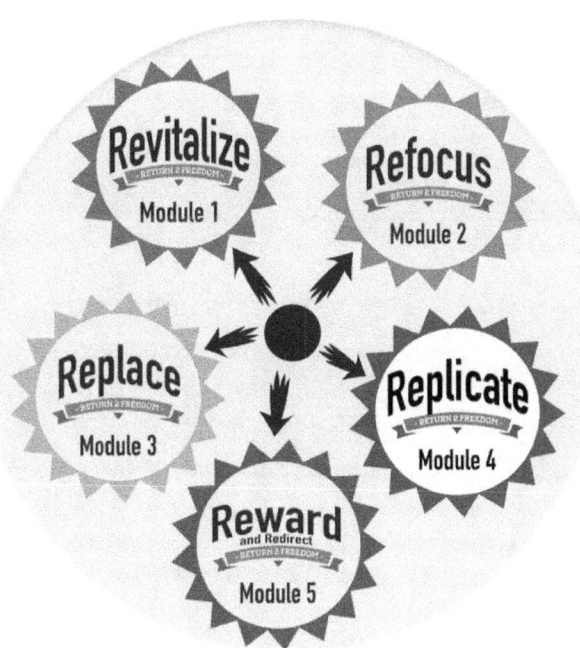

REPLICATE ~ COACHING YOUR LEADER

"I think what coaching is all about, is taking players and analyzing there ability, put them in a position where they can excel within the framework of the team winning."

DON SHULA

YOU ARE GONNA FLIP!

Because the mystery of coaching will disappear once you read this story.

I moved to Columbus, Ohio, to be with the love of my life. I came from a career in NYC, and if you ask my husband, he would tell you how much I love Manhattan: the museums, Central Park, the eateries and fresh markets...

In the interest of this story, it is good to note that while in NYC, I was part of the team that opened and introduced the Disney Stores to the Big Apple.

So, when I was hired by Starbucks and told they were opening a new market in Columbus, I was comfortable with what it would take: recruiting, and training, operational hurdles, construction and grand opening events.

But I'll fast forward here a bit to introduce you to Jen, the young woman who embodied coaching for me.

It all started in Dearborn, MI. I spent a few months with a training manager to learn how to run a coffee shop — the Starbucks way.

Now Jen was a superstar. A superstar knows how to run a shop and can draw out the best in her team.

Jen's store was an impressive working environment. The employees knew the expectations, followed through without hesitation, and tasks were completed. Even a task easily forgotten, like checking the bathrooms before and after breaks, was done by every employee.

Her staff loved working for her too. She was firm yet cheerful and often looked to have a good time. She loved her customers and enjoyed working with her employees or 'partners' as they are called at Starbucks.

And most impressive to me, was her willingness to 'roll with the punches' since she was given only a few days to prepare for my arrival.

After orientation and several days working in the store with her, Jen knew it was time to show me how to close the store.

On my first night closing shop with her team, she brought me over to the back room and said, "Okay, we're going to mop the floor." I, being eager to learn, watched and listened as she taught me how to mop the floor.

"We take the mop bucket and we put it into this little tub area to fill it with water. Add just enough soap, just a few dribbles because it's concentrated. You'll get a ton of suds if you add too much."

She then showed me how to wheel out the mop and bucket, how to lay down the first layer of soapy water, mop it up, rinse, and wring the mop until most of the water was out, and wipe down the same space with the wrung mop.

Next, it was my turn to perform the same steps. While I mopped, she watched and gave me feedback. When she was satisfied with my knowledge of how to do the task successfully, she left me to finish on my own.

This may sound silly, but from that point on, I was very confident and knew exactly what the expectation was when it came to mopping the floors.

I didn't have any questions. I understood how much soap and water to put in the bucket. I knew how to mop the floor and most importantly, I was able to teach someone else the way she taught me.

That, my friends, is the magic of excellent coaching! Every employee that received this type of training was not only confident to finish the task, but they were also successful in training others.

Now let's break down the steps of coaching so you can replicate them when training your leader to accomplish a new task.

Jen took the time to follow these steps each and every time she trained me on a new operation or task in the store.

Here's what she did:

1. *Communicated to me about what we were going to do.*
2. *Demonstrated how to accomplish the task.*
3. *Asked me to duplicate the process in front of her.*
4. *Gave me feedback on how well I did or what I needed to do differently.*
5. *Left me on my own when I was confident in*

my ability to perform it well.

6. *Allowed me to teach another employee.*

This model works because it uses all of the learning styles. We won't go too far into this here, but basically there are several ways in which people learn a new task. Some are audible learners, some kinesthetic, some visual….

The point is when you teach a new task, incorporate these multiple steps. Your leader will retain what they have learned and be able to replicate the process by teaching someone else.

This is exciting because you will only need to teach a task or function once, and your employee will then teach it for you after that. Woot! Woot!

Let us take a moment and review what typically happens in coaching. We will then see the contrast in the results.

What happens, all too often, is this:

The manager talks with a new employee, "Hey Joe, so this is your first night closing with us eh?" Joe replies, "Yeah." The manager brings him over to the back room and points to the mop bucket, "One of things we do at night is mop the floor, think you can handle that?" Joe nods his head and says, "Sure."

"Okay, then I'll leave you to it" the manager responds

and off she goes to do other closing duties. Meanwhile, Joe is left to figure out what she meant by 'mop the floor'.

We know what's coming next, a string of unfortunate events. Joe brings out a mop bucket filled to the brim with bubbles and water sloshing everywhere. The water is too soapy and everyone is slipping while they walk.

The manager tries to re-direct Joe on how to mop but feels too much time has already been wasted and now she just wants to do it herself. Joe feels utterly incompetent because he failed in this simple task of mopping the floor.

And everyone is scrambling to get the store closed because this whole episode threw a wrench into the closing duties.

There was needless stress created for all parties involved, simply because everyone was thinking, "How hard is it to mop the floor?" and no one considered the best idea, "Maybe we should teach him how it's done."

Take these coaching steps that I have outlined and use them with every task or duty. Sometimes it will only take 30 seconds to teach and other times an hour. Plan and schedule time to properly coach and teach your employees so everyone will win the end.

You may be surprised to learn, that coaching for

leadership behaviors is virtually the same as teaching a task. It's setting the expectation, showing or teaching what behavior is needed and providing feedback to help them be successful.

As long as you focus on the formula and repeat it on a daily basis, you will see a marked difference in the working environment when your employees are able to confidently accomplish priority tasks and behaviors.

With consistent coaching your mind will also start to automate the process and soon you won't even realize you are coaching anymore, as it just becomes second nature.

Your leader or manager will be more confident and capable in the tasks they perform and will then be able to take more things off your plate, which of course, will give you time to do other things.

All you will need to do in the future is follow up, and that takes us to our next step.

GO HOME

Step 5 ~ REWARD & REDIRECT

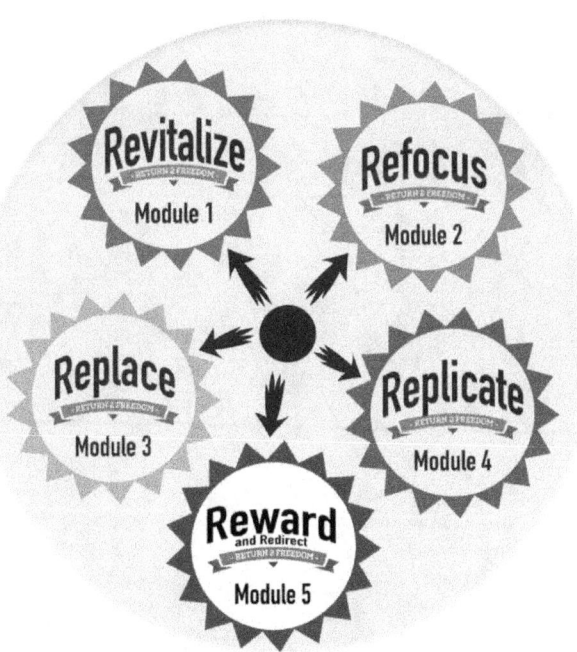

REWARD & REDIRECT - FEEDBACK FOR SUCCESS

"We all need people who will give us feedback. That's how we improve."

BILL GATES

What is Feedback?

Feedback is the praise or correction of one's behavior and performance. Learning to give valuable feedback is important, as once you have priorities set and coaching in place, you will no longer DO the things that need to be done.

Instead, you will observe others complete the tasks and give them appropriate praise or re-direction to be successful.

When you use proper feedback your team will know what behaviors are expected, how to perform their job more efficiently, and how to make decisions when you are not around.

So lets reveal how ongoing excellence is manifested with proper follow-up and feedback.

Are you ready for the secret?

Positive and corrective feedback cannot be vague. It must be specific.

One of the most common pitfalls leaders fall into when they try to provide feedback is that they are way too vague in their description of the behaviors they are addressing.

Here are some questions you can ask yourself to help you determine if your feedback is too vague:

1. Do you feel like you are constantly telling people what they need to change, but no one seems to do it?
2. Do you tell employees they did a good job expecting a repeat performance, but no such thing occurs?

If your answer is yes to either of those questions, poor communication and vague feedback may be the cause.

Here are two feedback models that will help you be most successful in directing or re-directing your team and leader.

They are:

Action/Benefit (positive).   **What action they did, why it was good, and the benefit of them doing it this way.**

Action/ReDirect/Benefit (corrective). **What Action they did, the redirect/what they need to do, and the benefit of doing things according to expectation.**

If the feedback is positive, use the Action/ Benefit model.

Action:
What they did.

Benefit:
Why it was good.

- Here's what you're going to do:

1) **Describe the specific behavior(s) or action observed.**

2) **Describe the positive impact it had on you, the team, and the business.**

This way they know exactly what they did and why it was so great. Here are two examples of effective and ineffective positive feedback:

Effective: "Sally, when you stopped and listened to that customer and found a solution to her request, you really showed her you were focused on her concerns and you probably made her a customer for life. She will also likely tell other people about how wonderful her experience was here."

Ineffective: "Wow, you did a good job with that customer."

Do you see how the first example is very effective feedback? It differs greatly from the second example, which is vague and non-descriptive.

Ineffective or vague feedback doesn't explain exactly what behaviors exceed expectations or how to replicate it. With effective feedback, Sally knows exactly what she did that was so great, why its important to the business, and how she can repeat it in the future. She also has more confidence that she is performing her role to expectations.

If you need to give corrective feedback, use the Action/ReDirect/Benefit model.

Action:
What they did.

Redirect:
What they should do.

Benefit:
Why change is good.

-Here's what you're going to do:

1) **Describe the specific behavior(s) observed.**
2) **Describe what behavior you expect in the future.**
3) **Explain the benefit or positive impact changing their behavior will have.**

This way they know exactly what they did, what to do differently, and why the change is beneficial. Here are two examples of effective and ineffective corrective feedback:

Effective: "Jim, when you arrive late to work it puts more stress on the staff and the customer service suffers. The expectation is that you arrive 5 minutes before your shift so you can be ready to help the team and give great service when your shift begins."

Ineffective: "Jim, hurry up and clock in. You're so lazy sometimes."

Once again, effective follow-up is specific and directed toward change as in the first example.

If Jim had been given ineffective or vague feedback, he wouldn't have known exactly what it was that made him 'lazy' and in turn he wouldn't know how to fix it. I know, you may think, "He should be able to figure it out."

But why leave it to chance? If Jim knows exactly what behavior needs to be changed, it's easier to make changes for the future. He will understand, and meet the expectations of his job.

The key to being successful is following up with consistent and specific feedback.

After a few months of working with a leader and giving them feedback, you'll find it easier to coach them to replicate these communication models with others. Employees will understand the expectations more clearly and receive communication in a positive and constructive way.

When employees know they are meeting the expectations it builds self-esteem. When you give good feedback, the end result is a more confident and capable team that enjoys their jobs and is willing to seek opportunities to go above and beyond.

Now and then however, there will be some tricky conversations.

There will be times when you hear about a behavior from a customer or employee that needs specific feedback, but you weren't there to observe it. To handle the situation effectively use these magic words:

"It has come to my attention..."

Then provide the appropriate feedback, using the Action/Benefit or Action/ReDirect/Benefit models.

If it's positive, the employee will be ecstatic that their good deed did not go unnoticed by the management.

If it's corrective, the employee will realize 'they've been caught'. Even though, the employee might be upset or embarrassed, it will allow you the opportunity to ask them to correct their behavior.

Those few words ('it has come to my attention') have helped me through many sticky situations where a behavior that I did not personally witness needed to be corrected. Despite there being no hard evidence in some cases, we often know reported actions are true because of previous behaviors.

Consequently, if a person continues to deny the

occurrence, it still gives you the opportunity to reinforce the expectations and thank them for their concern of being wrongly accused. Either way, you make your point and the person will have the opportunity to stop their behavior, or it just won't happen again not only because it wasn't true, but because they were reminded of your expectations.

Management takes discernment and when you can learn to decipher human behavior you will be able to understand situations even when you are not there.

We also know, as employers, sometimes it just doesn't work out.

You have provided help. You have given clear, consistent, feedback, and now realize this individual is not a good fit for your team.

Usually, when someone loses their desire to change or meet expectations it's because they are unfulfilled in their work. Their dissatisfaction can lead to team dissension and hurt the health of the business.

So, when it's time to part ways with an employee, even in this last conversation, continue to use the models we've discussed. It will help you address the situation without all the emotion that comes with an employee's lack of performance or bad behavior in the workplace.

First, these conversations should never be a surprise.

The last thing you want to do is have an employee blindsided by a pink slip. Instead, have in place systems to document previous conversations concerning feedback. This way, you can speak to those previous conversations and then explain how the expectations are still not delivered.

Approach the situation with a servant's heart and maintain the other's dignity. After all, they are people too. Sometimes they just need the right motivation to 'move on' and in this way you can help them out.

Give specific corrective feedback describing how they have not met the standards. If you can, point out dissatisfaction you have observed and the reasons why they may not be happy. They may realize it's time to go without more prompting from you.

Conversing with an employee in a respectful tone, giving proper feedback, and pointing out their unhappiness, will often move them to think about their situation and make a decision to voluntarily exit. For many reasons, including legal ones, this is often the best way.

Following this path will make it much easier for you to shake hands and part ways.

However, if you give vague feedback or usher them out of your business without explanation or blindside them, you will destroy your influence as a leader and the ability to have a positive effect on them even when they are not a good fit for your team.

On many occasions, I have had the unfortunate responsibility of 'letting people go'. Scott, a colleague of mine at Starbucks, once told me, "It should never be easy, Michelle. You should always have a pang in your stomach when you need to fire someone, because you have their livelihood in your hands."

These words have been a comfort to me and have helped me prepare in the right way to address uncomfortable conversations. Because of this approach, I have stayed in contact with former employees who were unhappy or not a good fit and have witnessed their excitement in a new job or new opportunities. Surprisingly, most of the time, they even remained loyal customers.

The main take away of this chapter is to remember to provide proper feedback by communicating your expectations clearly and helping your team to understand how they are performing in meeting these expectations.

With this whole process, you are teaching your employees how to be better leaders and decision-makers. In order to walk away from your place of business and go home, you want to feel confident your team knows how to make good decisions on your behalf when you are not around.

Take some time to think about behaviors you would like to see changed and then approach your employees and try it out. You may need to rehearse a little before you have the conversation, but in the end it will be easier than you think.

.

GO HOME

WHERE TO GO FROM HERE

"If you think in terms of a year, plant a seed; if in terms of ten years, plant trees; if in terms of 100 years, teach the people."

CONFUCIUS

You need people.

You need people who are good at performing day to day operations. You need people who embrace your values and want to uphold them.

You need people who make great decisions even when you're not around, so you can go home and live the life you've always dreamt of as an entrepreneur.

But let's face it, people are messy. It's not always easy to coach them and give feedback. At times, you may realize you have been working with an individual for months and are still not quite sure if things are going in the right direction.

You will have moments where you screw it up. There will be days you will feel as if nothing is working.

Get over it now because consistency is your lifeline.

When it comes to coaching people, consistency is implementing the steps to create success. The steps are simple but may not always be easy.

I promise that there will be a day when you can look back and see how far a person has grown since you started. That moment will give you the inspiration to continue and the reward for not giving up.

What excites me about training and coaching people is the idea that no matter where they end up, they have become better leaders to leave a legacy.

Instead of looking at a manager in training as someone to 'get the job done,' I desire to see those individuals grow their interpersonal skills, learn how to run a business and grow into great leaders. I know that no matter what industry they work in, the skills they learn to be a leader are transferable to any position they accept in their future.

I love seeing people develop their skills and maximize their strengths. They become so much more effective in overcoming challenges and can impact the world around them with excellence when given the opportunity.

And it's exciting to see!

You are not alone with this challenge.

It's because of the challenges we face when working with people, that when I thought about teaching this to others, I felt it was vital to have live online training and a community.

A community where people, like you and me, can go and ask questions and get others ideas, opinions, and advice. A community where people can help each other out and acquire aspiration to continue   - or work towards - their success.

My boss, Joe, used to say, "There are only two kinds of effort allowed on my team. Push Up or Pull Up." We can recognize another's success and push them up toward greater heights or lend a hand to pull those up that needed help. This is why my goal, for us and the community, is to find like minded people who see value in others and want to help everyone become more successful.

As an owner, you can provide the right environment for a leader to grow and thrive. You can give them the opportunity to ask questions, offer solutions and help them move forward even if they make mistakes.

This journey is rewarding. There will be awesome

highs and devastating lows. But in the end you will be closer to your dream of going home.

If you are looking to 'Go Home' with confidence and peace of mind and have a particular person in mind to receive training, go to return2freedom.info for information. You will learn how they can begin a path of personal growth and development that will give you more flexibility as an owner and them more confidence and knowledge in leadership.

If you yourself are interested in a personal plan for you and your business. You can contact me here: 1-404-586-4029 (US) Leave a message or press 1 to be directly connected to my personal line.

ABOUT THE AUTHOR

I grew up near the Rocky Mountains in Pueblo, Co. When I was in 5th grade my family moved to Denver and then we eventually landed on the East coast in Rockaway, New Jersey.

What I love about the East coast is the vibrant people and mix of cultures. NYC has always been a favorite stomping ground. After traveling with a mission group for two years, I began working with The Disney Store, and soon became a manager in NYC. It was a dream come true: I worked in the 'Big Apple'.

I was with Disney for almost 10 years and loved every minute of it. Disney was my first experience working with a world-class organization and in my opinion, I couldn't have learned from a better company about service, training and using the mission statement as a basis for making the right decisions on their behalf.

While working in NYC, I reconnected with the love of my life and moved to Columbus, Ohio. The move ended my career with Disney, but opened up another opportunity.

At the time, the Starbucks Coffee Company was just opening in Columbus and they needed experienced managers to train and develop people, open stores and build the brand in the area.

I was not only able to utilize learned skills, but I was exposed to another aspect of growing a business. At Starbucks, I learnt to put others first in the workplace as a servant leader, to utilize my strengths to benefit the team, and to exponentiate my own personal growth through consistent ongoing development.

The mentors and bosses I had with Starbucks took the foundation I was given at Disney and grew my potential ten fold as a manager and leader.

My time with these two organizations and the leadership within them set me up for continued success in working with people.

In 2007, I began working with my husband in his business of eight years and in 2009 created my own business and have been helping owners market themselves online ever since. Early in 2014 I had an "AH-HA" moment.

Business owners wear many hats and can't be good at wearing all of them. I am no different. However, one thing I've realized is that I have the ability to identify people with great leadership potential, train them toward success, and position them to be excellent managers and leaders.

Now my mission is to teach the principles I have learned in order to help others be able to live the life they dreamed of as an entrepreneur. The training is called Return2Freedom and includes online seminars, live events and a community of entrepreneurs dedicated to teaching leaders how to take their place.

I now live in Woodstock, GA. with my husband David, and our two kids, Sofia and DJ.

In addition to growing our own businesses, we enjoy sightseeing and swimming, foraging for new and interesting eateries, reading exciting books (our most recent series: Harry Potter) and living with our Husky, Shyla.

So, that's a little bit about me. I can't wait to hear about you.

RESOURCES

With the exception of personal friends and colleagues, all "Quotes" in this book came from brainyquote.com

Pg. 24 "create magical moments" — disneystores.com

Pg. 31 Nordstrom's commitment — nordstrom.com

Pg. 33 "Best 30 min. of a Child's Day" — disneystores.co.uk

Pg. 37 'Just Say Yes' policy — even though this is a well known policy, I thought I'd give props to this blog for the reference. http://www.carriedils.com/good-customer-service-skills/

Pg. 63 DISC test — the DISC test is offered as part of our R2F community. You can also find more info. here http://discpersonalitytesting.com

Pg. 73 Learning Styles - http://en.wikipedia.org/wiki/Learning_styles

If you haven't already...

Register This Book and Get Free Updates and Free Video Training

To get free video leadership training visit:
www.return2freedom.info
or
Text your name & email to
+1 (404) 586-4029
or
Scan this QR code:

GO HOME

Return2Freedom Online Training

Concentrated training in 5 areas for business owners and leaders. Learn & develop the essential skills of managing people and business.

R2F online community also offers: Live Seminars, Personality Tests, Personal Plan, Coaching Tools, Recommended Books, & Ongoing Development.

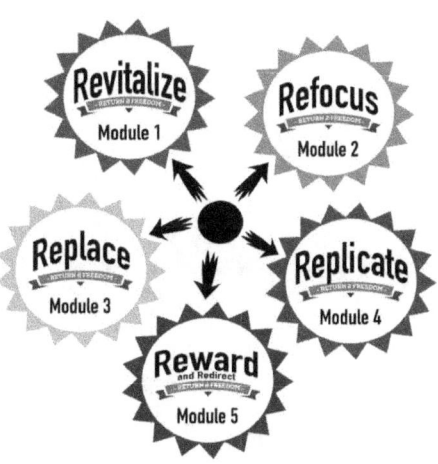

For more information visit: return2freedom.com